11497

Peoples and Nations of

ASIA

A short history of
each mainland country in Asia

Sheila Fairfield

Gareth Stevens Publishing
Milwaukee

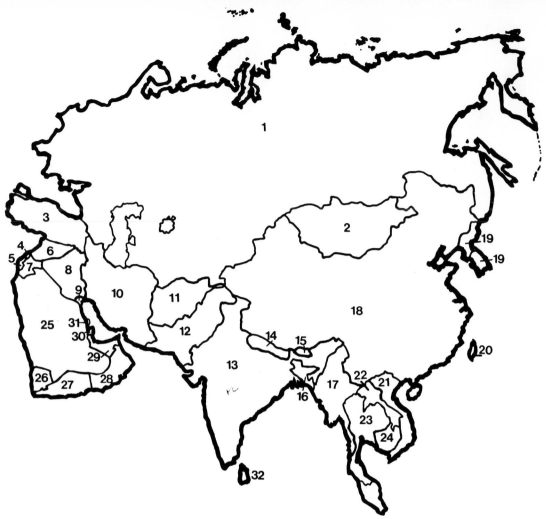

This North American edition first published in 1988 by

Gareth Stevens, Inc.
7317 West Green Tree Road
Milwaukee, Wisconsin 53223, USA

This fully edited US edition copyright © 1988. First published
in the United Kingdom with an original text copyright © 1987
by Young Library Ltd.

Designed by John Mitchell
Individual country maps by Denis Monham and John Mitchell
Full-continent map by Kate Kriege
Picture research by Sara Steel

1 2 3 4 5 6 7 8 9 94 93 92 91 90 89 88

Library of Congress Cataloging-in-Publication Data

Fairfield, Sheila.
  Peoples and nations of Asia.

  (Peoples and nations)
  Includes index.
  Summary: Presents a brief history of each
mainland country of Asia, from Afghanistan to
Yemen.
  1. Asia — History — Juvenile literature. [1. Asia
— History] I. Title. II. Series: Fairfield, Sheila.
Peoples and nations.
DS33.F34 198   950   88-42920
ISBN 1-55532-905-5

CONTENTS

A note on the entries in this book: Each nation-state and dependency has a written entry and its own map or a reference to a map elsewhere in the book. Also, some countries include lands that are geographically separated from the main area. These lands do not have a separate entry but are included in the main country's entry. Finally, some countries are mentioned that are part of other continents. They do not have entries here, but you can find them in other volumes of the *Peoples and Nations* series. Some Asian countries have their entries in **Peoples and Nations of the Far East & Pacific**.

TURKEY

Turkey is a republic that lies between the Black Sea and the Mediterranean. A small western part, including the ancient capital of Constantinople, now called Istanbul, is in Europe. A part in Asia, called Anatolia, has great plains, while much of eastern Turkey is very mountainous.

The first dominant people were the Hittites, who came from the north about 2000 BC and founded a strong kingdom. The Hittites had war chariots and were good at using iron. Once established in Turkey, they went on to conquer parts of Syria and, briefly, Babylon in Mesopotamia.

The next invaders were Phrygians. They had lived in Thrace, now in Bulgaria, and came across the Bosporus Strait. They then overpowered the Hittites, who moved south and regrouped in new city-states beyond the Taurus mountains.

On the west coast of Anatolia the Greeks established colonies. Some of these became famous in the arts of Greece, such as Aeolia for poetry and Ionia for philosophy. Inland, the Phrygians controlled the northwest and another group, the Lydians, controlled the southwest. Lydia became a rich territory, because there was gold in the Pactolus River.

In the far east, mountain people from northern Persia moved into the area around Lake Van. There they were attacked by Cimmerians, who swarmed down from the Caucasus mountains. After about 680 BC the

On the left is the famous Blue Mosque of Sultan Ahmed I, on the shore of the Bosporus.

The caves in these extraordinary limestone hills in ancient Cappadocia have provided homes for people for centuries.

Cimmerians moved on from their new Lake Van base and devastated Anatolia, which they controlled for forty years. Only the Greek colonies remained. Lydia, with its great wealth, managed to revive, however, and its king, Croesus, went on to gain much of Anatolia. He then took on the Persian empire — and lost.

Turkey was held by the Persians from 547 to 334 BC. However, Persia was eventually conquered by the Macedonian Greeks under Alexander, and his successors ruled for nearly 300 years.

Turkey now had many small states where the descendants of Hittites, Phrygians, Lydians, and Greek colonists went on living. Over all these groups was a Greek-speaking ruler, spreading a Greek culture, and old Greek cities like Ephesus and Pergamon flourished. When Celts, moving east from central Europe, came into central Turkey, the Greek cities were strong enough to keep them from getting any further, so they settled in Galatia.

In 113 BC the last king of Pergamon left his land to the Romans. By AD 14 they had most of the rest of Anatolia. Eastern Turkey was taken much later, but Roman influence there was never strong. The Romans felt more at home in the Greek cities, which went on being rich and successful until the next invaders came — the Turks.

The Turkish tribes came from the vast area which is now Turkestan in the USSR. Their homelands extended from the borders of Mongolia to the Caspian Sea, and they spoke the Turkish language. Some time after AD 1000 a tribal chief from Kirghizia, called Seljuk, was converted to Islam. His followers then moved into the great Muslim empire, which had its center in Iraq. They became its most powerful people and went on to conquer much of Anatolia in 1071. In the fourteenth century more Muslim Turks,

the Ottomans, replaced the Seljuks and conquered the rest of Turkey.

There was one nation, however, whom none of these invaders ever really controlled. The Muslim Kurds, a mountain people with a Persian language who still live in southeast Turkey, northern Iraq, and northwest Iran, lived by herding and by growing crops where they could. They were also feared as soldiers and resisted all

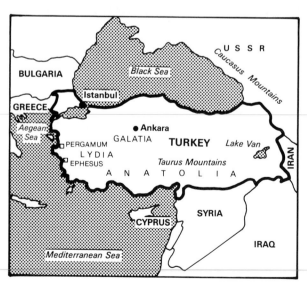

Istanbul lies between the Black Sea and the Mediterranean, and straddles Europe and Asia. This is a view of the European part in the 1890s.

invaders. Saladin, the Muslim commander who fought against the European Crusaders in the twelfth century, was Kurdish.

The Ottoman Turks went on to build a great empire. The eastern, Greek-speaking part of the Roman empire was still ruled from Byzantium (Istanbul), but by 1453 the Turkish sultan had taken Byzantium and also held many eastern European states. During the sixteenth century Turkish power spread along the Mediterranean.

The Turks had originally come westward through Persia from Turkestan. They had replaced the Persians as the greatest power in the Muslim world, but they still admired Persian culture until about 1600. By then Persia had adopted the Shiite form of Islam, while Turkey's empire was reaching centers of western thought. Therefore, there was conflict between the religions and cultural ideas of west and east.

Eventually, the empire was threatened

by its rival Russian and Austrian empires. At the same time, the Turkish government lost its grip on its local governors, whose rule over faraway provinces became harsh and greedy. There were revolts all through the nineteenth century, until the empire ended in 1918.

Turkey then appeared weak, but in 1919 Mustafa Kemal Atatürk started a movement to bring about a modern, reformed, strong, and Europeanized Turkey. This man's ideas affected justice and government, religion, the alphabet, and even dress. In 1922 the Sultan was deposed and Turkey, with its modern frontiers, became a republic.

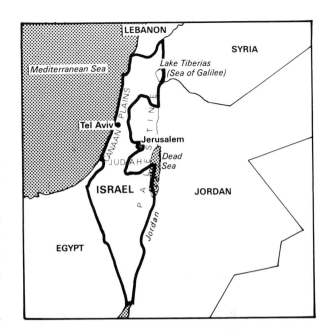

ISRAEL

The land between the Jordan River and the Mediterranean Sea used to be called Palestine. By 2000 BC, people from the north had settled to a civilized life in towns near the coast. Another group, the Hyksos, had brought their horses and great flocks of sheep to the other people of Palestine. They were farmers as well as shepherds.

The strongest nearby nation was Egypt. While the peoples of Palestine competed with each other and fought off smaller tribes, the Egyptians took control. Egypt was a rich country, and so the Hebrews moved there in a time of famine, and were held as slaves.

Egypt, too, had to defend against invasion. First, the Egyptians had to fight for Palestine against the Hittites, a strong people who invaded from Turkey and Syria. Later, in about 1200 BC, there was an invasion of people from the Aegean Islands. Among them were the Philistines, who made a kingdom in the south. While Egypt was weakened by invasion, the Hebrews escaped by 1200 BC and returned to Palestine to become its strongest people. They believed that there was only one God and that he had promised them the land of Canaan. They established the kingdoms of Israel and Judah.

Hebrew power lasted until 587 BC. Then their southern kingdom, Judah, was conquered by Babylonians from Mesopotamia, and Judeans (Jews) were deported to Babylon. During their exile they used the Aramaic language and kept it when they returned to Judah in 539 BC. They were able to rebuild their nation in spite of being ruled by foreign overlords — Persians, Greeks, and Romans. They also kept their Jewish law, customs, and religion, even though followers of Jesus of Nazareth, who lived in Judah during Roman occupation, founded the new religion of Christianity there.

Eventually, there was rebellion against

Roman rule. By AD 70 it had failed, and the Romans destroyed the Jewish state. Many Jews were killed and thousands were driven out. They settled throughout the Middle East, and their descendants spread worldwide, an event known as the Diaspora. Palestine was left to those Semites and Greeks who accepted Roman rule and to the desert tribes whom Roman rule did not affect very much.

In the fourth century the Roman Empire became Christian. Palestine was ruled from Constantinople, where the form of Christianity was Greek Orthodox.

However, Muslim forces from Arabia invaded in 636, and Palestine became part of the Muslim empire. In the eleventh century the Turks took over and ruled for 800 years until their empire collapsed during World War I, when Britain took control. The population at the time was largely Arab with some Jews. However, Jews from all over the world began migrating to Palestine because of its special place in their religious history. The Arabs wanted to stay for the same reason. In 1947 the United Nations divided Palestine into Arab and Jewish parts, but open warfare broke out. In 1948 the Jews created the State of Israel and revived the ancient language of Hebrew. Further wars have changed the borders of Israel and its neighbors, and parts of what used to be Jordan, Syria, and Egypt were taken by Israel in 1967. Modern Israel is a Jewish state, but Arabs make up a large minority of the population, and both Hebrew and Arabic are official languages of today.

On the left is the ancient city of Jerusalem, which is holy to Jews, Christians, and Muslims.

This mosaic picture-map in a Greek Orthodox church in Jordan shows Jerusalem in the sixth century.

The Koran tells us that Mohammed ascended to heaven from this spot in Jerusalem, where the mosque known as the Dome of the Rock is now standing.

JORDAN

Jordan is an almost landlocked country lying between the Jordan River and the Syrian desert. The one outlet to the sea is on the Gulf of Aqaba. Western Jordan has rocky mountains overlooking a flat, dry valley which contains the Dead Sea. Much of southern and eastern Jordan is desert.

In the tenth century BC Solomon, king of the Hebrews, ruled a kingdom which included west Jordan. The kingdom of Israel that followed Solomon's included northwest Jordan. The territory was victim to a series of invasions. In 733 BC Israel was conquered by the first of a number of invaders from the east, of which the last was Persia. After 323 BC, Persian Jordan was taken by the Greeks, who held it until it became part of the Roman empire in 63 BC.

None of these invaders, however, managed to control the desert, where the nomad families lived with their flocks. Nomads had nothing to offer invaders looking for profit.

Instead the conquerors preferred the north, where the Ammons had a town, Rabbath-Ammon, which the Greek rulers turned into a city called Philadelphia. In the southwest the kingdom of the Nabataeans, between the Gulf of Aqaba and the Dead Sea, was also worth taxing. The people lived off the trade route from Arabia to Syria and Lebanon. Their capital was Petra, a city cut out of the rock in a mountain valley.

The Romans made Jordan part of the Greek-speaking half of their empire. In Phildelphia there was some Greek culture, and Christianity came in the Greek Orthodox form, not the Roman Catholic. But

most ordinary people spoke Aramaic, a Syrian language, and had their own Christian church.

The Muslims of Arabia invaded in the seventh century, and many people were converted to Islam. Jordan slowly became a mainly Arab, Muslim place. In the eleventh century the Arab rulers were replaced by Turks. These Turks were also Muslims, but they did nothing for Jordan and its people, who were mostly Arab.

In 1915 there was a revolt against Turkish rule, after which Jordan was given to an Arab prince of the family that had led the revolt. He was Abdullah, son of Husayn ibn Ali of Mecca in Arabia.

Jordan, whose language is Arabic, is now a kingdom. Two wars with Israel have altered its western borders and have also brought many of Palestinian refugees to Jordan. Desert life survives, and new settlements have grown from phosphate mining.

The girl above is performing a folk dance in the colorful national costume of Jordan.

On the left is the Roman theater in Jordan's capital city of Amman, surrounded by modern houses and bustling, traffic-filled streets.

SYRIA

Syria lies on the upper reaches of the Euphrates River and southward into the desert, with a Mediterranean coastline. West of the desert are mountains sheltering the capital city of Damascus.

Syria has a variety of people. The desert people are nomads and always have been, herding camels, sheep, and goats long distances wherever there is a little water and grazing. Because they lie on the route from rich Mesopotamia (see entry for Iraq) to the Mediterranean ports, the cities have always had a mixture of people. City life was formed originally by ideas coming from

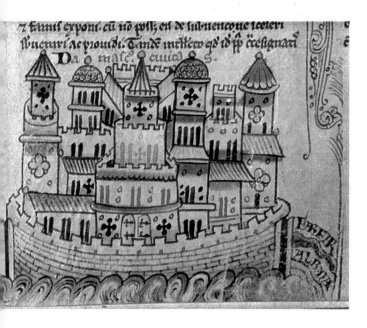

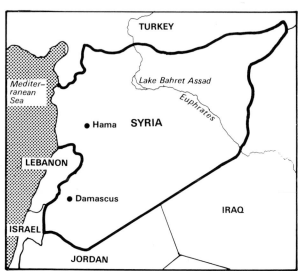

Mesopotamia along the trade routes. Syria's population also grew from invasion. The Hittites, a warlike, energetic Aryan people who founded a state in Turkey in about 1750 BC, spread into Syria. Later came the Hurrians, also Aryan, from the mountains of northern Iran.

For centuries the great powers of the Middle East — Hittites, Hurrians, Egyptians, and Babylonians and Assyrians from Mesopotamia — fought over Syria and its rich cities. By about 1200 BC southern Syria was Egyptian and the north was Hittite. Then the Hittite kingdom was destroyed by a sudden invasion by thousands of refugees from the Aegean Islands, the "Sea People." Chaos followed, and a group of desert people, the Arameans, were able to move in and found small states.

These Arameans gradually became the dominant people of Syria. The Aramaic language became common, spreading down the trade routes into other countries. The great power struggles over Syria began again, but the Arameans survived under Persians, Romans, and Greeks, although the Greeks had perhaps the most effect. ("Syrian" is a Greek word meaning "Aramean.") Eventually, Christianity came from Palestine before AD 100. A Greek Orthodox church supported by the government then developed, as well as native churches which the Greek church disliked and attacked.

One of Syria's greatest trade routes ran from Damascus southward to the western coast of Arabia. Arabians came to know about Damascus and its glories. In AD 636 they conquered it, and Syria became part of an Arab world. Many Syrians were converted to Islam, the Arabs' religion. Additionally, desert Syrians had much in common with desert Arabs, so for them these were the least foreign of the invaders. The Arabic language replaced Aramaic except in the surviving Christian church.

Damascus was the center of the Islamic empire for about 100 years. Under the next Muslim rulers, the Turks who arrived in the eleventh century, it slowly declined, because these Turks from central Asia were not Semitic like Arabs and Jews and so did not support the culture with the same interest. Turkish rule ended with World War I (1914-18). By that time Syrians were primarily Muslim, but many still held to Christianity and other faiths. Cities held Syrians, Turks, Arameans, and Greeks.

Syrian Arabs had fought hard for independence, but it did not come. Instead, France was put in charge of Syria in 1020, and independence was gained only in 1946.

SAUDI ARABIA

Saudi Arabia is a great, rectangular peninsula lying between Africa and the rest of Asia, with the Red Sea on the west and the Persian Gulf on the east. The Red Sea coast of Saudi Arabia is called the Hejaz, which has a narrow plain rising to hills inland. The central plateau of Nejd has three sandy deserts. The biggest desert is called the Empty Quarter.

The most important towns of early times were in the Hejaz. Mecca and Medina grew up as trading cities on the route from the Red Sea coast up to Syria. Besides lying on an important trade route, the Hejaz has fertile land, growing enough food to support city life.

Inland, past the hills, were Bedouins,

The heavy clothes and head coverings of these Arabs protect them from the piercing sun and dusty winds of the desert.

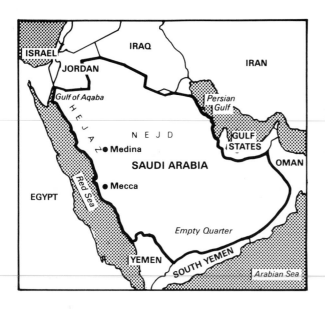

nomadic tribes who bred camels, sheep, and goats. They had to bear the flying, stinging sand, the terrible heat of summer, and the intense cold of winter nights. They fought each other and attacked anything worth looting. Their small groups were led by sheiks, who could rule as long as their men were willing to follow them. They roamed about the desert.

In about AD 543 the prophet Mohammed was born in Mecca. Many Arabs of Mohammed's time were not Jews or Christians, but he had met Jews and Christians in the Hejaz and studied their scriptures. The religion he founded, called Islam, is seen by his followers, called Muslims, as the final revelation of God's will.

Muslim beliefs brought the desert tribes together as a powerful force. By conquest and settlement they founded a vast empire throughout northern Africa and the Middle

East. However, the habit of arguing among the tribes revived, and two sects arose, Sunnite and Shiite. As the Muslim faith grew, Arabic, the language of Muslim scripture, spread widely, and Arab names were used from Spain to Afghanistan. The empire had a large navy, because coastal Arabs had always been efficient sailors and educated Arabs were famous for mathematics and astronomy — the two sciences needed for long-distance navigation.

Power in the empire eventually passed to Persians and then to the Turks who became overlords of the Hejaz in 1517. Both of these powers were Muslim, and Mecca remained important as Islam's holiest city.

The Sa'ud family were sheiks of all the Nejd by 1747. They joined the Wahhabi sect, which claimed to be the purest form of Islam. This sect became powerful when the Sa'ud took the Hejaz in 1925 and became kings of all Saudi Arabia in 1932.

Today the country has a rich oil industry that attracts many foreign workers and has even altered the life of the Bedouin through the oil profits they have made and their contact with western cultures.

LEBANON

Lebanon lies on the Mediterranean coast between Israel and Syria. Its coastal plain is narrow. Mount Lebanon, once famous for cedar trees, rises steeply inland. Behind Mount Lebanon is the Bekaa Valley, and beyond it are the Antilibanus Mountains, which lie along the Syrian border.

The first significant people were the Phoenicians, who built up Sidon and Beirut as ports. At times they were ruled by Egypt, but after about 1400 BC they became rich, independent people. The Phoenicians lived by sea trading and by hand-crafted goods. They were good at working in metal, glass, and dyes. They also bought and resold goods brought to them from Syria, Mesopotamia, and Arabia, and also set out on their own long trading voyages. Lebanon was conquered many times by Assyrians, Babylonians, Persians, and Greeks — all anxious to profit from its trade.

Lebanon became part of the Roman empire in 64 BC. By that time it had people from Mesopotamia and all from over the eastern Mediterranean. Many spoke Aramaic, a Syrian language, but educated people spoke Greek, the language of the last conquerors, and lived according to Greek ideas. The Romans admired these ideas and preserved them.

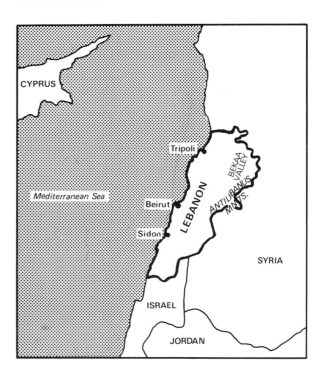

One of the few remaining cedars of Lebanon, growing over 6,000 feet (1,800 m) up in the snow-clad mountains. They have been famous since Biblical times.

When Christianity came to Lebanon from Israel, two churches developed: the Greek Orthodox church, supported by the Roman government, and the Syrian Maronite church, which disagreed with the Greeks about the nature of Christ.

In the seventh century the Arabs drove out the last Roman rulers and brought in their own Muslim religion. The Greek church became weaker, but the Maronites remained strong, especially in the mountain regions.

In the eleventh century another Syrian sect, the Druse, spread into Lebanon. They believed in one God who has lived on Earth several times. Like the Maronites, the Druse also settled in the mountains.

In 1516 the Turks, Muslims from farther north, took Lebanon as they conquered the enormous Islamic empire. Turkey held Lebanon until 1918, when France was given control after World War I.

During the last years of Turkish rule Christianity had flourished as a means of rebellion, further encouraged by French missionaries. When Lebanon became independent in 1944, the majority was Christian.

Power in government was shared according to religion. By 1960 there were many more Muslims in Lebanon, but their share remained the same, and their discontent grew into civil war in 1975. Additionally, Palestinian guerillas (see entry for Israel) began using Muslim neighborhoods in Lebanon as bases for attacks on Israel. Finally, Syria and Israel, together with several other political and religious factions, have joined in the fighting, creating a conflict that has proven difficult to resolve.

IRAN

Iran is a large country lying between the Caspian Sea and the Persian Gulf. The country is a plateau surrounded by mountains. Southwest of the Zagros mountains is a fertile plain watered by the river Karun. Here in about 3500 BC, the Elamites lived a prosperous life around their capital at Susa.

The Persians, or Iranians, arrived from the north about 1000 BC. They were an Aryan people like the people of north India. They settled on the plateau of Iran, but saw that better land than that on their dry plateau lay to the west. Therefore, their early emperors wanted fertile Mesopotamia and the rich trade that went through it to the coast of Syria and Lebanon. Cyrus the Great (600-529 BC) made many western conquests. In 549 BC he conquered the Medes, a people much like the Persians who had ruled an empire from what is now northwest Iran.

A sixteenth-century Persian picture of Tamerlane and his court. Tamerlane was the Mongol conqueror of most of southern and western Asia.

Later Persian emperors won an empire that reached from the Mediterranean to the Indus River and included Arabs, Jews, Medes, Baluchs, and Afghans, as well as Persians. The empire at times also included the Parthians, a warlike people known for their mounted archers, who lived to the southeast of the Caspian Sea.

The Persian empire was conquered in 330 BC, when the emperor reached too far westward and threatened the Greeks, who defeated him. But the Greeks could not keep the empire together. The Parthians revived and built up a vast kingdom of their own that lasted until AD 227. A time of revival then came for the Persians themselves. A new family of emperors, the Sassanids, took control, only to find themselves always at war with the Parthians and the eastern half of the Roman empire. The rulers and peoples of Persia became exhausted from all this fighting.

The people had mainly followed the religious teachings of Zoroaster, who lived about 800 BC. He taught that there is one good spirit, whose signs are light and fire, and one bad spirit, whose sign is darkness. Mithras, a god serving the good spirit, was worshipped with rites of fire.

In the seventh century the many tribes of Arabia were united by the new religion of Islam. They then attacked the rich centers of Mesopotamia and beyond, and by about 640, they had defeated the Persian emperor.

Persia then became part of the Islamic world, and Islam slowly replaced other major religions.

In time the Persians imposed their own high civilization on the world of Islam, which became filled with Persian art, music, and literature. Even Persian carpet designs showed the dream that first drew these plateau dwellers down to Mesopotamia: a beautiful garden, sheltered from the wind and watered by streams.

But more warlike people came from the northeast — the Turks and Mongols. In 1055, Turks conquered the Islamic empire of which Persia was part. They in turn were driven from power by the Mongols. Mongol

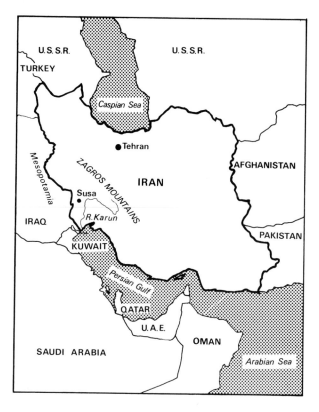

armies sacked the empire's capital in 1258. Eventually, they went on to conquer all Persia and held it until 1447.

Islam survived, and in 1502 Persia was conquered again by Turkestan tribes under Ismail Shah Safawi. A Shiite Muslim, he made his faith the state religion.

Persia now became different from neighboring Sunni Muslim states. Turks, whose nation was the strongest, did not like Shiite Islam. Their old admiration for Persia turned into hostility and rivalry.

Meanwhile, the Russians also wanted to use Persia to spread Russian power southward. In the twentieth century, when oil was found in Persia, the threats from stronger countries became worse.

From 1925 a new royal family tried to make Iran, as it was now called, stronger.

Their rule ended in revolution in 1979. The country is now a republic, ruled by Shiite Muslim clergy. Once again there is war between Iran and the owners of well-watered Mesopotamia, now called Iraq.

A variety of people now make up the Iranian population. Besides its ancient cities and the towns that grew from the oil industry, Iran has nomads. There are also the Kurds, a mountain people of northwest Iran (see entry for Turkey).

OMAN

Oman lies at the southeast corner of the Arabian peninsula. There is fertile land in the north, which is famous for its dates, and in Dhofar. From ancient times Dhofar produced frankincense, a valuable resin product. Dhofar was the center of important trade with Red Sea ports.

Oman has mountain ranges also. Barren Jabal al Akhdar lies west of Muscat, while Jabal Qarra in the south has rain on its southern slopes that provides pasture for

This group of young women is dressed in the national costume of Oman.

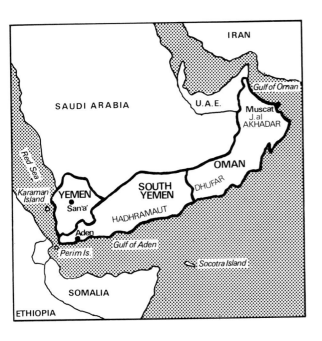

Then the tribes of inland Oman rose in revolt. They did not approve of hereditary rulers anyway, and they felt that the Sultan in Muscat did nothing for them. In 1913 it was agreed that the tribes should have their own imam, an elected Islamic leader. This arrangement lasted until 1970, when a new sultan took over the whole country.

Modern Omanis are still mainly Arab, although some Indians, Baluchs, Africans, and Pakistanis live in the ports. Oman also has an important oil industry.

SOUTH YEMEN

South Yemen lies on the southern coast of Arabia. It has desert and wild mountain country which is hard to live in. But it also has a long, sheltered valley called the Hadramaw. It is also home to the great port city of Aden.

Aden has always been important. From Aden ships could go across the Indian Ocean, up the Red Sea into Egypt, or down the east coast of Africa. People from all these places brought their trade to Aden, and the city had quite a mixed population.

The native people of South Yemen are Arabs. Those who were not merchants or fishers on the coast farmed in the Hadramaw or herded animals in the deserts and mountains. They were cut off from the tribes of north Arabia by the great desert called the Empty Quarter, and their dialects were different from northern Arabic. However, like the north Arabians, they lived as many tribes under sheiks and were converted to Islam in the seventh century.

In the sixteenth century the land was

cattle. Its northern slopes are desert, as is much of Oman.

The people of inland Oman are Arab tribes of two big alliances — Ghafari and Hanawi. They became Muslims in the seventh century and joined a Muslim sect which taught that rulers should be elected. In 1741 a ruler of the Al bu-Said family was elected. The family became powerful and managed to pass on the throne from father to son. They also won an important overseas empire when Omani rulers gained control of Zanzibar, in East Africa. From there they controlled much East African trade. Eventually, for better control of trade, Oman's capital was moved from the interior to Muscat on the coast.

In the nineteenth century European merchants wanted a share of this business empire. Portuguese, Dutch, and British traders all competed and set up trading posts. The Arab empire weakened when the British stopped the African slave trade.

conquered by the Turks. They were also Muslims, yet as an Asian people, they had little in common with Arabs. They concentrated on Aden and left the tribes alone.

In 1839 the British took Aden. They wanted it as a coaling station for their ships on the way to India. Britain held Aden until 1967. By that time it was one of many small territories forming the Federation of South Arabia. In 1967 there was a war of independence which was also a civil war with rival liberation armies. The Federation was destroyed, and the present country was founded as an independent republic. It includes the islands of Perim and Socotra.

YEMEN

Yemen is a small country located at the southwestern corner of the Arabian peninsula. It is a highland country with a narrow plain along the coast. Most people live in the hills as crop farmers.

Yemen was once part of a major trading area. The coastal cities dealt in goods from Africa, southern Arabia, and India. Spices, ivory, gum, and incense were all profitable. Unlike much of Arabia, Yemen had regular rain, and the people could farm by irrigation, growing enough food to make it possible for people to live in cities.

By about 700 BC Sheba, the most powerful local state, was setting up colonies on the African coast of the Red Sea. The people

On the left is Sana'a, probably the oldest city in the Arabian peninsula. The stone-built city stands high in the mountains of central Yemen.

On the right, a British-built fort stands on the citadel of Herat, on Afghanistan's Iranian border.

were Arabs, and claimed to be of two kinds: "pure" southern Arabs and later arrivals from the northern deserts. They shared their cities with foreign businessmen: Greeks, Jews, Egyptians, and Indians. Through them they heard of foreign religions like Judaism and, in time, Christianity.

Eventually the area lost its power. It was sometimes ruled by its African offshoot and then in the late sixth century by Persia. Finally, Arabs from farther north invaded Yemen, bringing their new Muslim religion. Yemen became part of a vast Arabic-speaking Islamic empire. The Arabian cities of Mecca and Medina, however, were the centers of Islam and became more important places than the Yemeni towns. Then the Yemenis adopted the teachings of one small Muslim sect, which separated them from neighboring Arabs.

In the twentieth century there has been revolution and civil war. Yemen became a republic in 1962. The state includes the island of Kamaran in the Red Sea.

AFGHANISTAN

Afghanistan is a big country which lies between the USSR, Pakistan, and Iran. In the north there are high plains near the Oxus river, bleak in winter but full of flowers after spring rain. In the south, sandy land has been irrigated from the Helmand river for centuries. Elsewhere, the mountains rise to the Hindu Kush range of the northeast.

The lushness of Afghanistan was an attraction for various people. The most dominant of these are the Afghans, who are of the group called Pashtuns. Pashtuns speak Pashto. They believe they are descended from Abdur Rashid, a follower of Mohammed, and that they migrated east from Arabia. There are also Persian-speaking people: Tadzhiks in the north and Hazaras, who are of Mongol descent. Finally, there are the Turkomans and Uzbeks, who came south from Turkestan in the USSR and speak Turkish languages.

These people were not united in one kingdom until AD 1747, although they had been part of an eleventh-century empire ruled from Ghazni. Turkish, Mongol, and Persian emperors had been overlords of parts or all of Afghanistan at different times.

While they were part of the Persian

empire, the Afghans had been converted to Islam. However, Persia was conquered by a new ruling family who brought in the very strict Shiite form of Islam. Nevertheless, Afghans kept to their old Sunni form. A Sunni Turkoman soldier, Nadir Shah, took Persia in 1736. Persians rejected his Sunni reforms, and he was executed in 1747. His commander, Ahmad Shah, then retired to Afghanistan, where the tribal chiefs elected him ruler.

The new country had little peace after Ahmad Shah's reign. Russia in the north, and later the British rulers in India, tried controlling this wild country that lay between them.

One important feature for both Russia and Britain were the Afghan mountain passes, especially the Khyber and the Gomal. These were ancient routes into India for trade or invasion, and both could be con-

From the primitive loom pictured on the right, the weaver will produce a rug fit for a palace.

Below, a camel caravan of refugees from the 1979 Soviet invasion of Afghanistan trudges toward the safety of the Pakistan border.

trolled from Kabul. Therefore, there were two nineteenth-century wars between Afghanistan and British India.

In peacetime the people farmed the fertile valleys and kept flocks on the high

pastures. They were also merchants, making long journeys into Persia and India.

An amir, or king, went on ruling until 1973, when there was a rebellion, and a republic was founded. In 1978-79 there were more upheavals. Finally, a communist government that was supported by the USSR came to power. However, not everyone accepted this, and fighting broke out. Soviet forces arrived in 1979 and fought with government Afghan troops against Afghan guerillas. In 1988 the Soviets began to pull their troops out of Afghanistan, and the two groups in Afghanistan began to argue over who would govern.

IRAQ

Iraq covers all but the higher reaches of the Tigris and Euphrates Rivers. In ancient times, this area was called Mesopotamia, meaning "the land between the rivers."

By 5000 BC there were people living in the marshes where the two rivers meet. They probably came from Iran. They built villages in the reed beds and went out by canoe to hunt and fish. Their houses were built of reeds, which were bound in tight bundles and used like beams of wood. There are still reed villages in modern Iraq.

Although Iraq gets little rain, the soil is very fertile when irrigated with river water. In time the people also learned how to drain some of the swamps and make them into crop land. This was the beginning of the splendid kingdom of Mesopotamia.

The Sumerians first ruled in the south,

perhaps as early as 4000 BC. No one is sure whether they were immigrants or descendants of the early marsh people. However, from 3500 BC there were cities like Ur, Uruk, and Eridu. Each city had its own god and was ruled by the god's most important servant. The Sumerians had the earliest form of writing and were clever artisans, lawyers, merchants, and scholars. Eventually, however, the cities became rivals and fought each other.

Meanwhile, new people arrived in the north. They were from the Syrian desert and belonged to the Semitic group that included Arabs and Jews. In Mesopotamia they learned the Sumerian way of life and founded a state of their own with a capital at Akkad. By about 2350 BC they had an empire that included Sumeria and reached from the Syrian coast into southern Persia.

Then came the Chaldeans, who ruled from Ur in the far south, until their city was sacked by Elamites from southwestern Per-

sia in 2000 BC. At the same time, Semitic Amorites, also from the desert, came into the north. They became known as Assyrians from their chief god and capital city, Assur. They too copied much from the south, where another Amorite group ruled old Sumeria from the city of Babylon, near modern Baghdad.

There were more invasions from east and west, because Mesopotamia was rich and the cities were attractive to mountain and desert nomads whose life was hard. City buildings were equally impressive, rising in steps to great heights, until they towered over the flat plains.

Finally, the Arameans, Semites from Syria, came in about 1100 BC. They spread their language throughout Mesopotamia.

Babylon and Assyria became rivals. After 1000 BC, Assyria conquered the empire and built a new capital at Nineveh, which is near modern Mosul. However, Assyria fell about 612 BC, and Babylon survived under its last powerful king, Nebuchadnezzar, who ruled from 605 to 561 BC.

Eventually all Mesopotamia fell to the Persians in 539 BC. Later it was fought over between Persians and Greeks, Parthians from northeastern Persia, and Romans. By AD 630, it was part of a Persian empire made weak by Roman attacks.

The Persians were an Aryan people from a mountain and plateau country. In Mesopotamia they ruled a Semitic, Aramaic-

speaking people who grew crops in the flat riverlands. Therefore, there were few natural links between rulers and ruled.

In 633-37 the Arabs invaded, united by their new religion of Islam. They found it easy to drive the Persians out. The Arabs moved into the cities and the irrigated crop land, where they became a ruling class. They did not try to get the people to convert to Islam. However, those who did convert had to join Arab tribes. These converts were never treated as "proper" Arabs and became disgruntled. Many joined a new Islamic sect, the Shiites, as a way of showing independence from the Arabs.

Persia became part of the Arabs' empire. The Persians who had been driven out now returned to Mesopotamia, where they turned Baghdad into an Islamic capital with a Persian culture.

In 1258 the Mongols invaded from the northeast. They caused great destruction.

Furthermore, they knew nothing about irrigation or agriculture, so crop growing failed. Iraq became a place of deserts, lakes, and marshes. Wandering shepherds took over. Many were Bedouins from Arabia. Their way of life, their language, and their desert tribal customs still prevail in Iraq.

The country was ruled by the Turks from 1534 to 1916, and under their leadership city life revived. In 1921 Iraq became a kingdom under European protection. In 1932 it became independent and developed a new oil industry. There was a revolution in 1958, and Iraq is now a republic.

Agriculture has revived since the revolution, especially in the irrigated land around the Shatt-al-Arab. However, dispute over this waterway has led to war with Iran.

Not all Iraqis are Arabs. The country has a variety of people. Among these are the Kurds, who have some independence (see entry for Turkey).

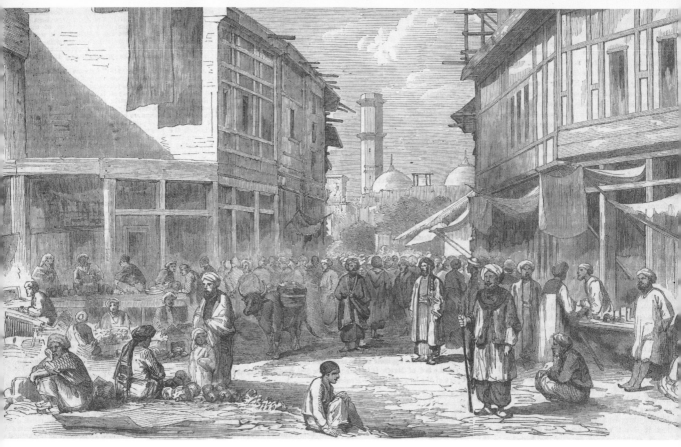

PAKISTAN

This is a street bazaar in nineteenth-century Peshawar, the gateway to the Khyber Pass.

Pakistan is bordered by India to the east, the USSR to the north, and Afghanistan to the west, and it has a southern coastline on the Arabian Sea.

The earliest important region was Sindh, the Indus valley, which was a rich, civilized place from about 2500 to 1750 BC. In 327 BC the Greek conqueror, Alexander the Great, invaded through the northern mountains. His small colonies left Greek traces on local art and language. On the other hand, Makran, in the southwest, was the "corridor" for incoming people from Persia and Mesopotamia. Arab sailors also arrived at the Indus mouth. During the eighth century AD they explored and occupied Sindh. Today

the Sindhi language is written by Muslims in a form of the Arabic alphabet, worked out while Sindh was an Arab Muslim state.

Pakistanis include Baluchs, Pashtuns, and Brahuis, as well as Punjabis and the people of Sindh. The Baluchs live in the hills and sandy desert of south Baluchistan. They are of mixed Persian and Arabic descent with their own language. Pashtuns live in north Baluchistan and the North-West Frontier province. They speak Pashto like the Afghans. Brahui speakers are a small group, related to the Tamils of south India who live in the southern hills.

The national language is Urdu, which developed under the Mughal emperors of

India as a mixture of Persian and Hindi. The Mughals were not the first Muslim rulers of the Indian subcontinent, but they were the most powerful. Muslim settlements had grown in the northwest from AD 711 through contact with Persia and Arabia, and under the Mughals, Muslims became a ruling class.

In the eighteenth century the Mughal empire was gradually replaced by British power. Muslim communities found it harder to keep their own kind of society intact, and there was always a resentment toward the dominant Hindu religion. When India became independent in 1947, it was divided in two states based on religion. The new Muslim state was called Pakistan.

This division created an upheaval. Many Muslims living in other parts of India set out for Pakistan. Hindus living in Pakistan moved out. The Sikhs of the Punjab had their state cut in half. There were often violent clashes.

Even more problems occurred because Pakistan was founded as two territories 1,000 miles (1,600 km) apart. East Pakistan had been the Indian province of East Bengal. West Pakistan had been the Indian territories of Baluchistan, Sindh, the North-West Frontier, and the western part of the Punjab. In addition, Kashmir was disputed between Pakistan and India, and in time Pakistan controlled part of it. Finally, in 1971 East Pakistan broke away to become the independent state of Bangladesh.

Today about eighty-eight million people live in Pakistan. The country is run according to Islamic law.

BAHRAIN

Bahrain means "Two Seas." Its islands lie with the Gulf of Bahrain on one side and the Persian Gulf on the other.

In the sixteenth century Bahrain was an Arab sheikdom and an important trading port. It was also one of the main sources of pearls brought up by divers. This rich place attracted the Portuguese. By 1521 they had control and held it until 1602. Bahrain was also at times held by the Iranians, and there were often fights with nearby sheikdoms.

By 1800 the British were powerful in India. Because the Persian Gulf lay on one of the main routes for the British East India Company, the Company began to "police" the Gulf with its own warships. Bahrain occupied a strategic location in the Gulf.

Therefore, in 1816 Britain and Bahrain signed a treaty which gave Bahrain British protection. This arrangement lasted until 1971, when Bahrain became independent again. The state now has oil, modern industry, and a big foreign population.

KUWAIT

Kuwait is a small state at the northern end of the Persian Gulf. There is Kuwait City and a mainly desert area inland.

The modern city was founded in the eighteenth century by an Arab tribe, the Anaiza, from the desert. It became the main trading port and marketplace for the northern Gulf. Pearl diving was important, as well as fishing.

The British East India Company arrived in the northern Gulf in the 1770s. Trade from the Gulf to Indian ports was an important part of their business, and they wanted the best base. Therefore, the British were active in Kuwait through the next century, and Kuwait was a British protectorate from 1899 until 1961.

Now oil is more important than trade, and Kuwait's oil wells make it wealthy.

UNITED ARAB EMIRATES

The Emirates lie on the Persian Gulf north of Oman. There are seven very small states: Abu Dhabi, Dubai, Sharjah and Kalba, Ajman, Umm al Qawain, Ras al Khaimah, and Fujairah. The states are desert except for some oases, and the sea was always the main provider of wealth until oil was found.

The people are Arab Muslims. Each state has its own emir as ruler.

Because Europeans were interested in Gulf trade from the sixteenth century, there

were many clashes between freebooting Arab captains and European ships. The Europeans called the area "The Pirate Coast."

In 1820 the British made a truce with these seven states, calling them afterwards the "Trucial States." In 1971 the states decided on their present union.

The Kuwaiti shopkeeper on the left is using the centuries-old art of plaiting palm leaves to make mats and baskets.

Falconry is still a popular sport over most parts of the Arabian peninsula. The hunter on the right lives in the oil-rich Arab country of Qatar.

QATAR

Qatar occupies a small peninsula on the west coast of the Persian Gulf. The people are Arab Muslims. Some came from the Arabian deserts farther west, while others have always been based on the coast as fishers and pearl divers.

After the sixteenth century Qatar was part of the Turkish empire, but the Turks made little impression on it. In 1916 the Turks left, and Qatar signed an agreement with the British. The country accepted British protection and agreed to stop Gulf pirates operating from Qatar bases.

Qatar became completely independent in 1971 and is ruled by an emir. It has an oil industry and many foreign workers.

INDIA

India stretches south from the Himalayas, forming a great peninsula into the Indian Ocean. Like all big countries it has many different peoples, languages, social groups, and ways of life.

Northern India has a plain watered by the Ganges and the rivers flowing into it. By 1000 BC this plain was being settled by an Aryan people who came from the grasslands beyond Afghanistan. They crossed the mountain passes and found land which was good for their cattle. Their descendants became the people of separate kingdoms, and their language became the source of the main north Indian languages: Hindi, Bengali, Gujarati, Punjabi, and Marathi.

South India is a plateau with some fertile valleys, but it also has forest and jungle. The coast and valleys were settled by people whose languages are called Dravidian. They probably came along the coast of the Arabian Sea from Persia and Mesopotamia. Their language has since divided into Tamil, Telugu, Malayalam, and Kannada.

All these people held or adopted the Hindu religion. The gods of Hinduism stand for the great forces: creation, destruction, generation, protection. There is also an elaborate system of customs for daily behavior, and there is a "caste" system. Caste separates society into priests, farmers, warriors, artisans, and so on, grading their importance from the priests, who are the top caste. The separate castes have their own parts in the gods' scheme and must keep themselves pure without mixing castes.

Gautama Buddha did not approve of caste or powerful priests. He founded Bud-

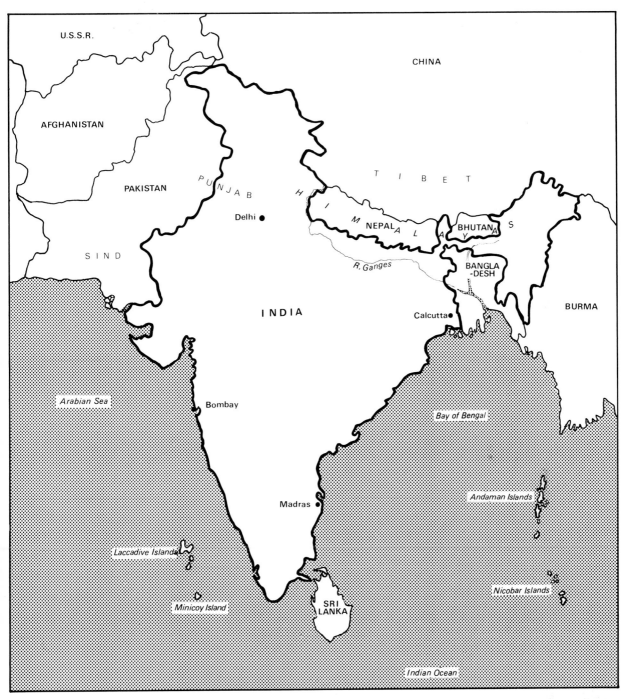

U.S.S.R.

CHINA

AFGHANISTAN

PAKISTAN

P U N J A B

Delhi •

S I N D

H I M A L A Y A S

T I B E T

NEPAL

BHUTAN

R. Ganges

BANGLA -DESH

INDIA

BURMA

Calcutta •

Arabian Sea

Bombay

Bay of Bengal

Madras •

Andaman Islands

Laccadive Islands

Minicoy Island

SRI LANKA

Nicobar Islands

Indian Ocean

Sikhism blends ideas from both Hinduism and
Islam. This modern Sikh temple is in Delhi.

31

dhism as a reformed religion in India, although it is now much stronger in other southern Asian countries. Buddhists train their souls to perfection, although the soul may go through many human lives on the way. Another reformer of that time was Mahavia, who founded the Jains, or "conquerors of self."

There were always many small tribes in India that were neither Aryan nor Dravidian. Some of them survive today. Tribes are linked by family ties, not by caste. They live by hunting or hill farming. Some have adopted the Hindu way of life or that of the later arrivals, the Muslims.

Arab merchants began setting up trading colonies on the west coast after AD 650. In 712 there was an Arab state in Sindh, now in Pakistan. By 1000, Islam had spread from Arabia eastward, across Persia, to reach a Turkish people settled in Afghanistan. Their ruler invaded northwestern India and began conquests which his successors carried

on for 200 years. In 1206 they founded a powerful sultanate at Delhi.

At that time there were many states in India. Nobody had ruled all India since the Emperor Asoka died in 232 BC. The Delhi sultans were sometimes able to wield real power over the Rajputs and other strong Hindu rulers and sometimes not. In far eastern India there were mountain warlords whose tribes resembled the people of Burma or Tibet. They took little notice of Delhi.

In 1526 Babur, ruler of Samarkand, conquered Delhi and became the first of the Mughal emperors of all India. *Mughal* means "Mongol" in Hindi. Babur was descended from Genghis Khan and Tamerlane (see entry for Mongolia), but his people were generations away from the first, fierce Mongolian cavalry. They were still soldiers, but they were used to ruling a civilized city with a Muslim faith and Persian culture. These Mughals valued the beauty, art, and fine handcrafts of India and added to them. They even produced a new language, Urdu, combining elements of Persian and Hindi.

Also at this time the Sikhs broke away from Hindu and Muslim teaching to develop their own beliefs, blending ideas from both religions. Their founder was Nanak (1469-1539). By 1764 the Sikhs had achieved their own state, Punjab.

In the eighteenth century the Mughal empire was dying, just at the time when

European countries were competing for Indian trade. Merchant companies were able to take control of the areas where their goods came from. The Portuguese had had bases on the west coast from 1498, but the British and French newcomers became much more powerful. They fought each other and the Indian rulers who, with no strong emperor in Delhi, found it difficult to protect themselves. The British East India Company controlled huge areas of the country by 1857. In that year there was an uprising, and a new kind of government had to be found. The British government took control of the Company's territories and made new agreements with states where Indian princes ruled.

States under British rule became much more Europeanized than the others. Christianity, Roman Catholic or Protestant, came with the Portuguese, French, and British. English, like Urdu before it, became a standard language of trade and politics used by many whose native languages were too different to communicate otherwise. Many British settlers came to work in the army, the civil service, trade, or the tea industry.

In the twentieth century there were two movements which grew rapidly. One was for independence and the other was for a separate state for Muslims. In 1947 India became independent, and the separate Muslim state of Pakistan was created. This partition involved thousands of people in long migrations and many clashes at the time, although Muslims in India today outnumber the population of Pakistan.

Since independence India has become a republican union including all the former princes' states. New state borders have been made, grouping people mainly according to language.

India also includes the Andaman and Nicobar Islands and the Lakshadweep group (Laccadive and Minicoy Islands) in the Indian Ocean.

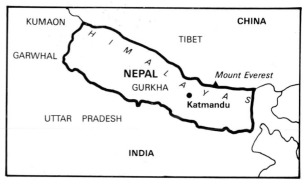

NEPAL

Nepal is a kingdom in the Himalaya Mountains. It is enclosed on three sides by India and on the fourth to the north lies the Chinese province of Tibet. Among the northern mountains is Mount Everest, the highest in the world. In the south great forests slope down to the jungles of the Indian border.

The original people were of the same group as Mongolians, and they arrived in the mountains from the north. Refugees from India came later. They were mainly Rajput warriors and their followers, driven into the hills by wars.

For centuries there were many groups of tribes and small Rajput states. In 1559 one of those states, Gurkha, in central Nepal, became a strong kingdom. In the eighteenth century the ruler of Gurkha was able to spread his power through what is now Nepal. The name "Gurkha" is now used to describe people from all parts of the country. The main language is Gorkhali, spoken by the descendants of the Rajputs and written in an Indian alphabet. The other language is Newari, which developed in the Katmandu valley. The states of Newari people there were conquered by Gurkha in 1769, but the language survived.

Rajput descendants are Hindu, but Buddhism survives also. Buddha himself was born in Nepal in 563 BC. His teaching spread through India and back into his birthplace. It was adopted by many of the mountain people, including the Sherpas.

"Sherpa" means "man from the east." The Sherpas are a Mongolian people who settled in Tibet and then moved into Solo Khombu in northeastern Nepal. They are farmers and herdsmen who also work as carriers in the mountains and serve many Himalayan mountaineering expeditions.

Gurkhas formed a distinctive unit of the Indian Army during the British rule of India, but Nepalese never became part of the British empire. People of Nepalese descent also live in two parts of the Indian state of Uttar Pradesh, called Garwhal and Kumaon, which belonged to Nepal before 1816.

BHUTAN

Bhutan is a very small kingdom in the Himalaya mountains, lying between eastern India and Tibet. The north is high and cold, with snowy peaks, while the south is warm and wet. Its thick forests and jungles have always been a fine defense.

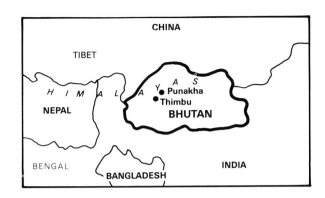

The people follow a form of Buddhism which came in from Tibet in the twelfth century. Their language is Dzongkha, whose speakers at first lived in scattered villages, herding animals and growing crops wherever they could. They were rather like the people of Tibet, because they had similar customs and there was no firm frontier between them.

In the eighteenth century Bhutan was in danger from both sides. In India the British East India Company gained control of Bengal to the south, while the Chinese gained control of Tibet to the north. The people of Bhutan were invaded from Tibet many times. It was not possible for isolated villages to put up a strong defense, so they made themselves into a union with one ruler. Once this had been done, the ruler could cope with the British by making a treaty with the Tibetans and by building forts, which are called *dzongs*. They are built into the mountainsides, high up, overlooking and protecting the valleys. They became the centers of the only built-up places outside the capital, which was then at Punakha. The dzongs are the size of small hill towns. The various districts of the country are still administered from them.

The power of Chinese Tibet faded, but that of India grew stronger. The rulers of Bhutan made more treaties with British India, and even while both countries are now independent, their economic ties are very strong. English is used as an official language, as it is in India. Nepali, which has spread along the Himalayas from further west, is also spoken.

These Bhutanese children speak Tibetan at home, but at school learn English from a teacher born and trained in India.

35

BANGLADESH

Bangladesh is a small country enclosed on three sides by India and with a coastline broken up by the mouths of the Ganges River. It is in Bangladesh that this great river is joined by the Brahmaputra. The abundance of water has brought as many difficulties as benefits: floods, steamy marshes, and shifting channels. But where there is crop land it is very fertile, producing rice, fruit, vegetables, and jute, a long-stemmed plant that breaks up into strong fibers.

The people are Bengali. They are one of the nations descended from Aryans who moved into India from central Asia before 1000 BC.

The Bengalis' state was called Bengal. It was divided between West Bengal (mainly Hindu) and East Bengal (mainly Muslim, and more rural than the west).

The rivers could support a large population with many towns and villages. There was great competition for livelihood, and Bengalis became known for their quick minds. Various rulers of India found them

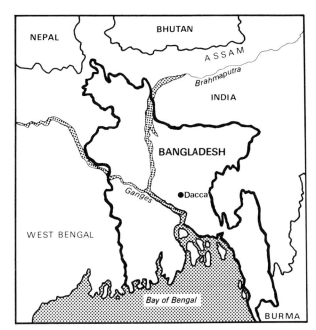

This 1200-year-old building in Bangladesh is thought to be the oldest Buddhist monastery in the world.

to be efficient and employed them, especially in Assam, as officials. So the Bengali people spread.

In 1947 India obtained its independence from Britain. Many Muslims wanted a state of their own, and so Pakistan was created (see entries for India and Pakistan). West Bengal remained part of India, while East Bengal became East Pakistan. There is a great distance between East and West Pakistan and no real link between the two except religion. In 1971 civil war broke out, and East Pakistan broke away to become the independent republic of Bangladesh.

SRI LANKA

Sri Lanka is an island lying east of the southern tip of India. Most of its inhabitants are descendants of people from India. One group, the Sinhalese, Aryan people from north India, arrived before 500 BC. Their language developed from Sanskrit.

The Sinhalese adopted Buddhism in about 250 BC during the reign of the Buddhist emperor of India, Asoka. When Asoka died, there was trouble in India, and another wave of emigrants left for Sri Lanka. These were the Tamils, a Dravidian people from south India. Their Tamil language was one of a south Indian group, and they were Hindus. They settled first on the Jaffna Peninsula, and then spread south. From the beginning there were wars between Sinhalese and Tamils. These wars continued, on and off, for centuries.

Sri Lanka has two monsoon winds bringing rain: the southwest, which comes every year, and the northeast, which is unreliable. In the southwest and central hills, crops grow with natural rainfall. But in the north and east, rainfall must be stored and distributed through canals. The early Sinhalese kings had vast irrigation systems built, and the northern plains produced plenty of food. The people paid for their own land by helping to build and repair the many different dams and channels.

King Parakrama Bahu the Great united Sri Lanka, kept out invasions, and irrigated great areas. But when he died in 1186, the state broke up, the irrigation systems fell into ruin, and the Sinhalese moved to the southwest to grow crops.

The first Europeans to arrive were the Portuguese in 1505. They found several kingdoms and Colombo, center of the southwest, as the main town. The Portuguese, and the Dutch and British who followed them, built up cash crop industries with

On the left stand a group of Sri Lankan officials at a state ceremonial in Kandy in 1876.

On the right is a group of servants belonging to a Burmese noble of the mid-nineteenth century.

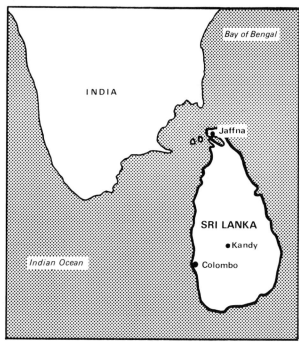

plantations reaching up into the central hills. The last Sinhalese hill kingdom, Kandy, was conquered in 1815-18.

Sri Lanka, which the British called Ceylon, was a British colony from 1802 to 1948. Foreign rule produced a foreign culture, and differences between Tamils and Sinhalese became less important than European-style education and ability in the tea industry or the civil service. There were arguments about preserving the Tamil language, but no open wars. After Sri Lanka's independence, however, the interest in national cultures revived. The Tamil-Sinhalese hostility has since reappeared, and some Tamils want to go back to the days of separate states.

BURMA

Burma lies on India's eastern border. It is a country of hills and jungles around big river valleys. The main river is the Irrawaddy.

By about AD 400 there were four dominant groups of people: Mons, Arakans, Shans, and Pyus. The Mons lived around Thaton and Pegou. From there they spread upriver and southeastward. Mon culture resembled that of their Indian trading partners from the Coromandel Coast of eastern India, except that Mons were Buddhists and not Hindus. The Arakans lived in the southwest, divided from the rest of the

beliefs, as did the Shans and Karens.

The Pyus' kingdom lasted until 832, when they were replaced by the Burmese. The Burmese came from the borders of China and Tibet and settled at Pagan by 849. They also conquered the Mons, but at first they admired Mon culture and adopted it. By 1174, however, Burmese national feeling had grown strong, and Mon ideas were

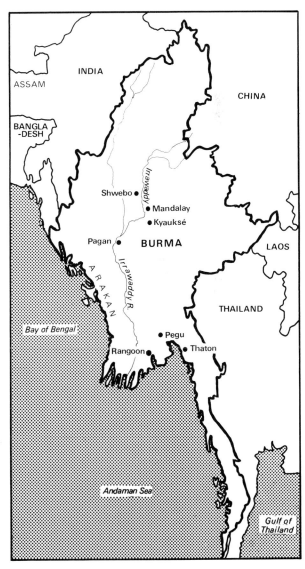

country by mountains. The people had frequent contact with India and may have descended from Bengalis. They were merchants, sailors, and pirates. Shans were tribes of warriors from the northern and eastern hills. They were T'ai people, like the Thais and Laotians. They lived by hill farming, raiding, and slaving. The Karens of the southeast were a similar group.

The fourth group was the Pyus, who came from the north to settle on the Irrawaddy below Shwebo. The Pyus were highly civilized and flourished on the irrigated rice fields which the Mons, who were excellent farmers, had made around Kyaukse. The Pyus came to rule much of south Burma, including the Mon states. They adopted not only Buddhism, but also Hinduism, and they kept some animist

dropped. Burmese, not Mon, became the official language.

War broke out often between the Burmese and the Shans, Thais, the rulers of China, the Laotians, and rebellious Mons. Therefore, borders often changed.

Portuguese traders arrived in Arakan in the sixteenth century. Their descendants formed a Roman Catholic settlement in the northwest. Some Portuguese became pirates and slave raiders, attacking the coast of Bengal in India. This led to war between Bengal and Arakan. During the war, Arakan declined into chaos. In 1785 Burma was able to conquer it.

After 1794 Arakanese refugees were pouring into British-ruled India, chased by Burmese forces. In 1822 Burma also invaded Assam north of British territory. There was war. The British took parts of south Burma in 1826 and the rest in 1852. They developed Rangoon as a port, shipping teakwood from the forests. The kings of

Burma still ruled the inland country, the first land they had held in Burma, from Mandalay, but Britain annexed this too in 1885.

Burma was attached to British India, but this did not succeed. Burmese customs of government were neglected, and the Indian systems did not work. Resistance went on until Burma was separated from India in 1937. During World War II Burma was occupied by the Japanese, but in 1947 the country became independent.

The non-Burmese people are still important. There are Shan and Karen rebellions. Buddhism is still the main religion.

LAOS

Laos lies along the Mekong River, between Vietnam and Thailand. There is fertile land in the river valley, while much of the rest is forest-covered mountain land.

Small groups from nearby states had moved into the southern hills and up the Mekong by AD 500. The dominant Laotian people, however, were T'ai, like their neighbors in Thailand, who came from Yunnan in southwest China. Their small states in northern Laos were united in 1353 into a kingdom. The king was related to the king of Cambodia, and his people had natural links with the people of Thailand. Buddhism and a culture modeled on Indian ideas came to Laos from these places.

Laos became a market for surrounding countries. Merchants from Thailand and

In Laos, as in much of southeast Asia, Buddhist monks in yellow or orange are a familiar sight.

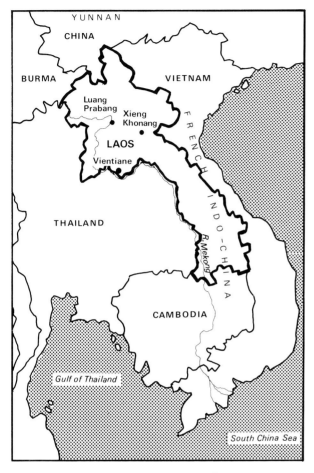

Burma came to meet those of China and Vietnam. There were two centers of power, Luang Prabang and Vientiane, which were sometimes rivals and sometimes united. Around Xieng Khonang was the tiny state of Tran Ninh, which paid tribute to Laos and to nearby Vietnam.

The greatest Laotian king was Souligna-Vongsa (1637-94), who united the country and kept it prosperous. Europeans, who were looking for Asian trade at the time, did not disturb Laos, because the Mekong was difficult for their ships and Buddhism was too strong for their missionaires.

The king, however, became disliked in Tran Ninh. After that Tran Ninh was willing to help enemies of Laos. By 1707 the country was divided into two hostile kingdoms, which were both conquered by Thailand in 1778. In 1827 there was a revolt. The Thais put it down by devastating the Vientiane kingdom and deporting the people. The rebel ruler of Vientiane fled to Vietnam for help. Now the Vietnamese saw their chance to win Laos and sent an army to help him against Thailand. But Tran Ninh captured the king and handed him over to Thailand. The Vietnamese were furious and took over Tran Ninh.

Rivalry between Thailand and Vietnam went on with Thailand still holding Laos until 1893. Trouble was made worse by raids from refugee Chinese rebels.

By 1896 France held Vietnam and claimed that Vietnam had a right to Laos. Eventually, Thailand lost Laos to the French, and the country was part of French Indochina until 1954. The communist Pathet Lao party had fought against the French, and after independence, went on fighting a civil war against the Laotian rulers. Both sides had foreign help. The Pathet Lao won. In 1975 they set up a communist government.

KAMPUCHEA (CAMBODIA)

Kampuchea (Cambodia) is a country of forests, rivers, and rice fields, with a short coastline on the Gulf of Thailand.

By AD 250 Funan, a state in south Cambodia, stretched down the Mekong Delta to the sea. Funan was a watery country. The cities had houses built on platforms with canals instead of roads. The marshes were drained into huge lakes, and rice fields replaced the marshes. The people

On the right is the Khmer temple of Angkor Wat, in the ancient ruined city of Angkor in Kampuchea.

were Malays, who traded across the Gulf to the Isthmus of Kra. That was the meeting place for merchants from India and China. Therefore, Funan ideas on kingship and religion came from India.

In northeastern Cambodia were the Lin-yi, or Cham, people from what is now South Vietnam. They were of Indonesian stock. In northern Cambodia and southwestern Laos lived the people who conquered Funan. They were called the Khmers.

By 627 the Khmers had Funan, called "The Water Kingdom," and shortly afterwards the rest, called "The Land Kingdom," of what is now Kampuchea. The Khmers also copied ideas from India. King Jayavarman II made a Hindu cult into the state religion. The king was godlike, and the state's well-being depended on the safe-

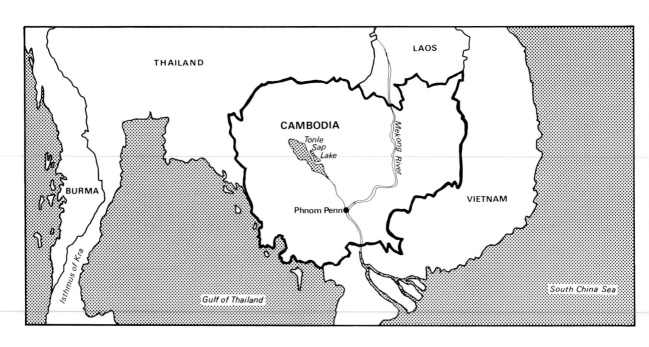

keeping of the sacred symbols in their shrines on the temple mountain.

The people worked at building great temples and on the irrigation canals and reservoirs from which they produced rice and fish. Their own religion was a mixture until about 1250 when a new type of Buddhism came from Sri Lanka. This became the people's religion. It did not teach that the king was godlike. As a result, royal authority became much weaker.

At the same time, Thais and Chams became rivals in trying to conquer Cambodia. The Thais succeeded in 1594. Then northern Vietnam joined in. Cambodia slowly died while wars and civil wars dragged on. By 1758 Vietnam had the Mekong delta. In 1845 it was agreed that Cambodia should be protected by both Vietnam and Thailand. However, by 1864 the French held southern Vietnam, and they persuaded Cambodia to accept French protection instead. The country became part of French Indochina and was for a time much safer. Independence came in 1953.

Then Cambodian communists, the Khmer Rouge, tried for power, helped by communist rebels from South Vietnam. There was civil war,. By 1975, the Khmer Rouge had won. They then began to turn Cambodia back into a peasant country. People were driven out of the cities to live in the fields if they knew how to farm, or to die there if they did not know farming. In 1977 the Khmer Rouge fell out with the Vietnamese, who invaded and set up a government, renaming the country Kampuchea. By that time much of the country's way of life had been destroyed, and it will take many years to rebuild.

THAILAND

Thailand, once called Siam, lies around the valleys of the Chao Phraya and the Mun rivers in southeast Asia. It also has a long "tail" reaching down the Malay peninsula.

The Chao Phraya valley was colonized before AD 550 by the Mon people, who also settled in Burma. They had an Indian type of culture, and at one time they were ruled from Funan in Cambodia, where Indian ideas were also popular. By about 650 there was an independent Mon state called Dvaravati near the mouth of the river.

The peninsula had many small states important on the trade route from India to China. They also had been held by Funan and were free by 600. But in 1050 Cambodia reconquered the south of Thailand.

In the thirteenth century new people appeared in the north, the T'ai, who came from Yunnan in southwestern China. In 1253 they were driven south when the Mongols took China. They then attacked the Cambodians and made their own states in Thailand. Chieng Mai was in the northwest. The kingdom of Sukothai was founded near Phitsannlok and spread east and south. By 1290 it controlled Dvaravati and much of the Mekong Valley.

The T'ai had a feudal society. However, they took ideas of art and government from Cambodia and copied their laws and Buddhist religion from the Mons. All this they expressed in their own T'ai language. They were advanced and civilized, but fierce. Their enemies, the Cambodians, called them "syam" — "savages."

About 1350 there was an upheaval. A new T'ai state arose in Ayut'ia in old Dvaravati and absorbed Sukothai. There was now a powerful country, united except for Chieng Mai, which became the cause of

In Thailand every young man becomes a monk for a few months. On the left, friends and relatives offer presents and flowers at an ordination.

Fruits and shellfish on sale at the early morning floating market in Bangkok harbor.

wars among the T'ai, Burma, and the Shan people of the Burmese hills. War between Thailand and Burma was also frequent.

In 1602 the Dutch began trading in Ayut'ia, and by 1665 had gotten control of the country's economy. The king allied with France, trying to balance Dutch power. The alliance led to military occupation. Then there was trouble with Britain about

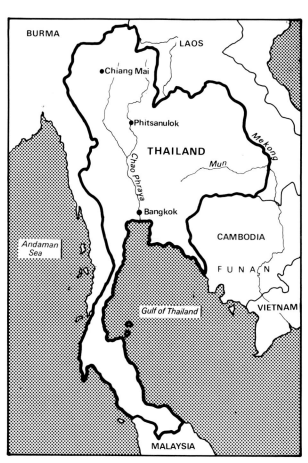

piracy in the Indian Ocean. Altogether, Siam's contact with Europeans was unhappy, and the country became strongly anti-European.

In 1851 King Mongkut came to the throne. He believed that European ideas should be allowed into Siam, but with the T'ais firmly in control. There were many changes, and more were made under his successor, Chulalongkorn (1853-1910).

The country's name was changed from Siam to Thailand in 1939. The opening of trade has brought much American and European interest, and there are large Chinese business colonies in the cities.

TAIWAN

Taiwan, a large island off Fukien province on the east coast of China, also includes two small islands, Quemoy and Matsu.

Taiwan's first people were southeast Asians from the same racial group as the people of the Philippines. Their descendants still live in the mountains and forests.

Chinese have been crossing to Taiwan for centuries, but especially after 1684 when it became part of Fukien province.

The Japanese held Taiwan from 1895 to 1845. They modernized it but did not settle there. In 1949, at the end of a civil war in China, about two million Chinese from the losing side came to settle in Taiwan and set up a government. At first there was friction between the islanders and the newcomers but things have since improved. All Chinese agree that Taiwan is part of China, disagreeing only on which nation is China's legitimate government.

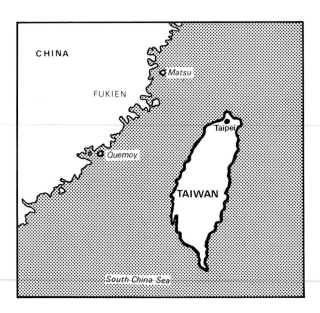

VIETNAM

Vietnam curves down the coast of the South China Sea, east of Laos and Cambodia. In early times the southern tip was ruled from Cambodia and the rest from China.

In AD 192 the state of Champa, south of Hue, broke away and became independent.

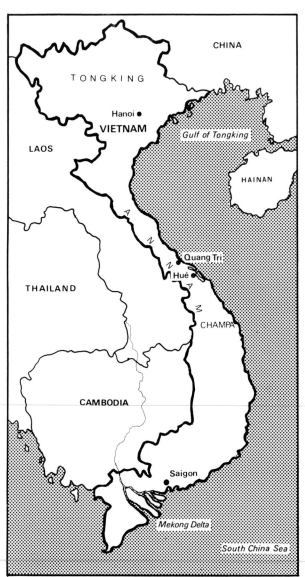

Men and women equipped only with pick and shovel dig out a great irrigation canal near Hue.

The Cham were of Indonesian stock, and they adopted the Indian culture which Indonesia was then copying. Also, in their northern towns, they learned about Buddhism which had spread down from China.

The Cham often fought on their frontiers with the Chinese provinces of Annam and Tongking. In 939 these provinces became the independent kingdom of Dai-co-Viet. The Viet people, who intermarried with local Lo and Annamites, were of Mongol type with a Chinese culture. There were also Chinese colonists. Taoism and the teachings of Confucius, as well as Buddhism, had many followers.

Wars between the Cham and the Viet finally led to the Cham defeat of 1471. The victorious Viet now ruled, governing through warrior clans who sometimes fought among themselves. By 1592 there were two powerful Viet groups. The Trinh ruled the north from Hanoi, and the Nguyen ruled the south from Quang Tri. By 1760 the Nguyen had taken the Mekong Delta, where Chinese settlers lived, as well as the Khmer region of the neighboring country of Cambodia.

Then civil war broke out among the

On the left is the Palace of the Throne in the seaport town of Hue in South Vietnam.

In the picture on the right, the British plenipotentiary in China makes a flamboyant entry into Beijing at the end of the third Anglo-Chinese war.

Below, a Chinese fisherman in the territory of Hong Kong spreads his nets in the shallow water.

Nguyen. A French Roman Catholic missionary gave help to a Nguyen prince, who agreed to accept French support in return for giving the French trade and military bases. With this support the prince won his war and also conquered the Trinh in 1802. He ruled as emperor, and the French had great power while he lived. In 1820 there was a new emperor who distrusted the French and persecuted Christians. French Catholics were killed, and France attacked. Southern Vietnam fell by 1862, and the north fell by 1885.

The north was always more anti-French than the south, and the most effective resistance group was Ho Chi Minh's communist party, begun in 1930. During World War II (1939-45), Japan invaded Vietnam and drove out the French, but the communists fought the Japanese. By 1945 the communists controlled the north, calling it a republic. When the French returned to rule the south, the communists sent forces against them and also helped communist rebels inside the southern state. In 1954 the south became independent. War broke out again in 1960 with foreign help to both sides. In 1975 the north won, and Vietnam became a single state with a communist government.

CHINA

China is a huge country stretching from a cold, bleak north to a tropical south, and westward from the China Sea into central Asia. The first Chinese lived in a small area around the Huanghe, or Yellow River. Their great lords lived in walled cities, while farmers and peasants grew wheat, corn, and vegetables. The people, through their priests, worshipped the spirits of their ancestors and of nature.

To the south and east were many groups of non-Chinese people who were small land holders, fishers, or hunters. In the hills west and north were herders like the Tibetans and nomads, such as the Turkish peoples and the Mongols, who were splendid riders. The Chou, nomads from the west, conquered the Chinese states about 1028 BC.

The Chou did not turn those states into a nomad world. They moved into the walled towns, and their warriors became landowners. They built new garrison towns to control the country, supported by the peasants who grew the food. The Chou were religious but did not employ priests. However, they saw that Chinese priests could read and write and give useful advice on local customs, so they used them as advisers and called them scholars.

China had no frontiers. The central ruler had full authority over the great lords near to him and less over those farther away. So the farthest off were able to build little empires of their own among the nearby people. Some of these people took to the Chinese way of life, while others kept their own ways and imposed them on the Chinese who had tried to absorb them. There

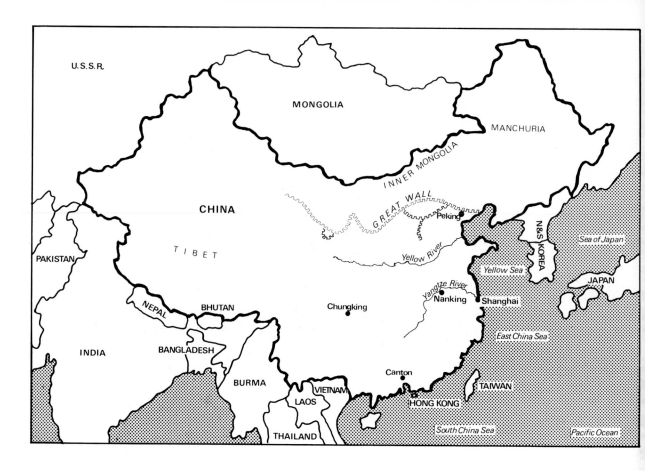

was often trouble in the north when the Chinese wanted more crop land to support their people and the nomads wanted the same land as pasture.

After a rebellion in 771 BC came the first of times when the emperor, the central ruler, lost his real power to the commanders and other leaders with their scholars.

Confucius (551-479 BC) was one of these advisers. He taught standards of correct behavior for the ruling families who employed him: value people according their age, rank, or position in the family and rule justly or you forfeit Heaven's good will. After 200 BC this teaching was made into a formal system by which a new ruling class

tried to live. They were called the "gentry."

Gentry families had country estates where they lived on rent from tenant farmers. Their sons were trained as government officers. They developed a powerful network of families that would be important in China for centuries.

Meanwhile, there were thinkers who disagreed with Confucius. Taoists believed that people should leave society to live in harmony with the natural world. Legalists believed that teaching on "good" or "bad" behavior was useless. Instead, they believed that the ruler should make laws to cover all cases, and that everybody should obey the ruler's laws without question.

This is the Great Wall built to defend China against ancient invaders. It is 1,400 miles (2,250 km) long.

The Buddhist religion came in from India some time before AD 1, took hold among non-Chinese first, and then spread. Chinese Buddhism was much affected by Tibetan Buddhism, a very strong, monastic religion, where the monks, called lamas, were Tibet's most important people.

China was sometimes one big empire and sometimes pieces of an empire that had broken up. States formed in the south when Chinese arrived looking for more land or were driven south by northern wars. They mingled with the original people, sometimes copying them, sometimes being copied. Good southern land produced rice, not wheat, so as more people moved south, rice became the diet of most Chinese.

The north was often invaded by powerful neighbors, some strong enough to conquer all of China. The Mongols from the north held China from 1280 to 1368, and the Manchus from the northeast held it from 1644 to 1911.

For centuries the flat-bottomed, square-sailed ship known as the junk has plied the seas around China, and is still widely used.

The picture on the right shows people of Seoul in 1758, when Korea was still controlled by China.

The Chinese had blood links with northern and western neighbors and also saw their strength. They acknowledged them as "brothers," but foreigners from farther away were despised. The Chinese were seldom good at foreign trade, because they expected foreign merchants to be suitably humble. They were seldom prepared for hard bargaining and often lost.

In the nineteenth century European traders, especially British and French, fought for and won trade agreements that were very bad for China. The peasants, always poor, became desperate. At the same time their leaders had the chance to study European ideas of government. All this caused discontent with existing conditions. This discontent grew into rebellions and finally into revolution. In 1911 imperial rule ended, and a republic was founded.

Tibet, a Chinese colony since 1720, again became an independent country. The Buddhist monasteries took up their old governing power, and the Dalai Lama, or "Living Buddha," was the head of the state, as well as head of Tibetan Buddhism.

The new Chinese republic split, with northern and southern governments, rival armies, and political parties. The new, small middle class was interested in Marxism, but Marxism was for industrial countries, and there was much argument about whether it would work among peasants. In 1921 Mao Zedong and others founded a communist party. At first they worked with the People's Party, or Kuomintang, but then quarreled. The communists had to escape, moving across China on the "Long March," during which many died. In 1937 Japan invaded China and occupied it until the end of World War II.

In 1945 the USSR supported the Chinese communists in a civil war. In 1949 the Kuomintang were defeated and withdrew to Taiwan. The communists founded the People's Republic of China, and in 1950 they reconquered Tibet.

There are still about sixty different peoples living in China and many different ways of speaking Chinese. (See also entry for Taiwan.)

KOREA

Korea is a small, mountainous peninsula, lying between China and Japan.

The Chinese established colonies in Korea by 100 BC, although most of Korea was in three kingdoms, which were often at war. The kings and their nobles protected the people with troops and fortresses, and the people paid with heavy taxes. One kingdom, Silla, in southeastern Korea, finally conquered the others and then drove out the Chinese in AD 676.

The kings of Silla tried to replace the warlords with a government run by civilians. On the whole the new idea was a success. There were enough periods of peace for the study of Buddhism and of the Chinese teacher Confucius, and for art and writing. The Korean language was then a spoken language only, but its sounds could be written down in Chinese characters.

There was always a shortage of good land. Most of it belonged to a few great landowners, whom farmers paid for the right to live and work on their land. The farmers also had to pay taxes and do military service. They became so discontented with this arrangement that they would not fight when the Mongols invaded from the north. So by 1260 the Mongols were the new overlords of Korea. They had also conquered China, so Korea was now linked to China and remained so for 700 years.

Chinese art and learning were copied until some scholars feared that native Korean arts would be forgotten. They did what they could to revive them, inventing a

On the left, Korean folk dancers perform an athletic dance to the beat of their unusual hourglass-shaped drums.

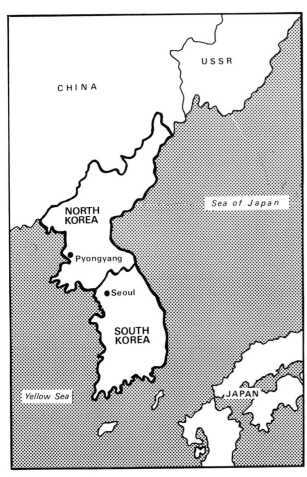

new, separate Korean alphabet in 1446.

The system of holding land was finally changed. Good farming became much easier, and the country became prosperous.

In the eighteenth century missionaries came, bringing Roman Catholicism. Some scholars were interested, but there were people who feared that foreign ideas could be harmful. This fear always grew worse in times of hardship. Since prosperity did not last because harvests were sometimes poor

and taxes were high, by 1870 many Koreans were afraid of all contact with foreign countries. Most of all, they feared Japan.

China and Japan were old enemies, and Korea was often caught between them. Japanese power over Korea increased, and Japan finally took control of Korea in 1910. Many Koreans escaped to China or Russia, where in time they adopted communism.

In 1945 Japan was defeated by the United States at the end of World War II. The Americans went into South Korea and supported a new government. Japan's other enemies, China and the USSR, were already in the north, supporting a communist government there. Each claimed to be the true government of Korea, and in 1950 they went to war. The war ended in 1953, and they agreed to live as separate and independent countries. Neither could develop their industry and trade without help from their allies. North Korea relies on China and the USSR, while South Korea relies on the United States.

UNION OF SOVIET SOCIALIST REPUBLICS

The Union of Soviet Socialist Republics, usually called the Soviet Union or USSR, covers all of northern Asia. It also extends west into Europe, where it includes Estonia, Latvia, Lithuania, Belorussia, Moldavia, and the Ukraine. There are about 276 million people, about half of whom are Russians.

The Russians are an eastern Slav people who settled in the forests of the west between AD 500 and 800. South of them were nomadic tribes, who were often at war. North of them, Vikings from Scandinavia, who the Russians called Varangians, were trading along the Volga and Dnepr rivers and making small colonies.

In 862 a Varangian leader, Ryurik, ruled in Novgorod. The Russians were being threatened by Turkish people from beyond the Caspian Sea, so they asked Ryurik for help. He became the leader of a Russian-Viking union which, in 882, moved its capital to Kiev.

In 989 Prince Vladimir of Kiev adopted Greek Orthodox Christianity as the state religion. This faith had reached Kiev through contact with the Greek-speaking half of the late Roman empire, but Russians were able to worship in their own Slavonic language. The empire included many Slavs. During the ninth century, St. Cyril had worked out an alphabet for writing scriptures and church services in the Slavonic languages.

In about 1220 came another wave of Turkic invaders, the Mongols, who lived north and west of China. By 1247 they had conquered Kiev and received tribute from Novgorod and the north.

Mongols who settled in the USSR are sometimes called Tatars. The vast crowds

Above is part of the extraordinary and beautiful Cathedral of St. Basil in Moscow, built by Ivan the Terrible in the middle of the sixteenth century.

There are hundreds of races in the many states of the USSR. The drawings on the left, of Samoyeds in the Lower Yenesei River region of Siberia, were made in the nineteenth century.

of mounted Mongol soldiers, and the families, herds, and portable villages that came with them, were called hordes. An important group which settled on the lower Volga was called the Golden Horde, and they were the real Tatars. There were many hordes, however, who covered the land from the Ukraine to the borders of China.

Mongols were raiders, not civil servants. They wanted tribute and obedience from conquered states, but they did not want to have to run them. And although most Mongols in time became Muslims, they did not want to interfere with the Greek Orthodox Church, which reached them through their conquest of Persia and of the Turkish peoples of Central Asia. As Muslims, these Mongols were different from eastern Mongols, most of whom became Buddhist.

In 1320 the Lithuanians invaded from the northwest and took Kiev. They went on to hold the Ukraine and Belorussia, where they ruled Orthodox Russians, Tatars, and Lithuanian and Polish settlers. Today Belorussians are part Lithuanian with their own language. Modern Ukrainians are more of a mixture, because their rich land attracted most of the Russian invaders in turn.

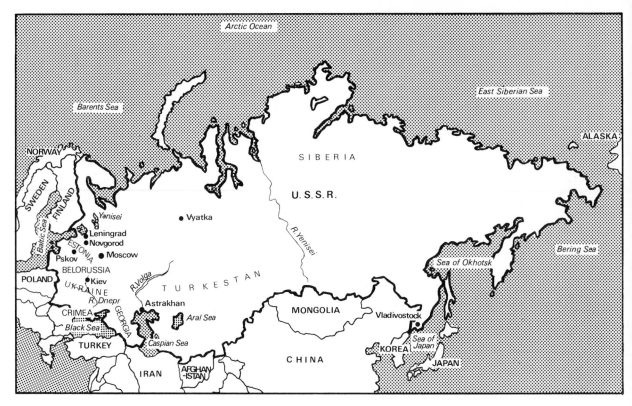

The Mongol empire began to break into small states, each under its own khan. Separate groups and the Turks they had conquered became the founders of Turkmenistan, Kazakhstan, Uzbekistan, and Kirghizia. Other khans ruled the Crimea and Astrakhan.

By 1460 the country was made up of Mongol lands, the Lithuanian empire, and some strong city-states like Novgorod, Pskow, and Vyatka. There was also Moscow, a powerful Russian trading center on a network of rivers.

Under Ivan III (1462-1505), Moscow invaded nearby states. The conquest of the great rival, Novgorod, was savage. By 1600 Moscow, called Muscovy in Europe, reached from the Arctic coast to the Caspian Sea and almost as far east as the Yenisei River.

Muscovy's style of government was not like that of the khans or the city-states where warriors or citizens had some say. In Moscow all power was in the hands of the ruler, the tsar. He had advisers to whom he did not have to listen. As Moscow's power spread, more people were brought under this rule and lost the importance they used to have.

Tsar Peter the Great (1682-1725) moved Russia away from traditional Asian ideas toward those of Europe. This caused a great upheaval, but it did nothing to lessen the tsars' power.

By 1884 Russia had almost reached the modern frontiers of the present USSR. The people on the frontiers of Turkey and Iran (Georgians, Armenians, Azers, and Tadzhiks) had been included in the tsars' empire.

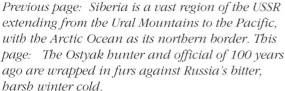

Previous page: Siberia is a vast region of the USSR extending from the Ural Mountains to the Pacific, with the Arctic Ocean as its northern border. This page: The Ostyak hunter and official of 100 years ago are wrapped in furs against Russia's bitter, harsh winter cold.

Most people were peasants, and there were many serfs who belonged to the landowners who employed them. Serfdom had existed in Kiev. However, in Moscow it became widespread because it provided reliable labor for the great lords who held all the frontier land and had to defend it all.

Neither peasants nor serfs could have challenged the power of the tsars, but educated people, who felt that they had the ability to govern, resented it bitterly. There were some reforms — for example, serfdom had ended by 1866 — but not enough. Rebellions led to revolution in 1917 and a communist republic founded under Vladimir Lenin (1870-1924).

Lenin taught that revolution had stages. First, industrial workers needed to be organized by full-time revolutionaries, so that they could overthrow the industrial world that employed them. Then the workers would become powerful rulers, just as the tsars had been. But this would not be necessary for long, and the last stage would be a world of equal people who did not need a state to control them at all. This has not yet happened in the USSR — or any other communist country.

The Soviet Union's empire was completed at the end of World War II. Several countries of eastern Europe previously under German occupation were turned into communist states and brought under varying degrees of Soviet control.

Communism does not recognize religion, but the Greek Orthodox faith survives. So does Islam in the south.

MONGOLIA

Mongolia is a high, cold country north of China. The Gobi, which is a cold desert, covers the south, and the Altai mountains cover the west. The rest has high, grassy plains and forests.

The Mongols are largely nomads, using fast, tough ponies to move about with their herds of cattle, sheep, and shaggy, two-humped camels. The traditional house, a round tent covered in warm felts, called a *yurt*, can be be carted about on a low wagon from place to place. Since animals need a lot of food when it is very cold, the herds move over vast areas of pasture in the harsh climate.

From the earliest times Mongols competed with neighboring people for grassland. At such times the herders became

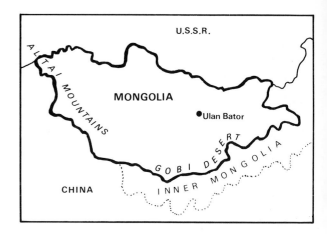

mounted soldiers, tough enough to cover the longest distances. In AD 1206 one leader managed to unite them and was given the title Genghis Khan, "Ruler of All." He led the Mongols into a great empire stretching across Asia into western Russia and south to China. Genghis Khan's grandson, Kublai Khan, became emperor of China in 1280. Kublai Khan's grandson, Tamerlane (1335-1405), ruled an empire from Samarkand. There are still many people of Mongol descent in China and Russia.

At first the Mongols had their own gods. There was a supreme god, and others, like Nagatai, who watched over a family, its herds, and its crops. But Tibetan Buddhism was widespread at the time of the Mongol conquests, and it became the main religion of the Mongol people.

Mongol power eventually faded, and Mongolia was in time conquered by China in the early eighteenth century.

In 1911-12 during a revolution in China Mongolia declared itself independent. There was argument over who controlled Mongolia until 1921, when Inner Mongolia remained part of China and Outer Mongolia became the present independent republic.

Under Soviet and communist influence Buddhism was suppressed in 1932. When this happened, many Mongolian Buddhists fled into neighboring China.

Karakorum was the capital of the Mongol empire. In this picture of the city can be seen a castle, a church, several boats on a river, and an inn. It all looks very European, and must have been painted by someone who had never seen it!

GLOSSARY

Aryan: A race that speaks one of the Indo-European languages; this group of languages includes most European and many Asian ones.

British India: The parts of India and Pakistan that from the mid-eighteenth century to 1947 were under British rule.

Buddhism: The religion founded in India by Prince Gautama, called Buddha, in the sixth century BC. It has spread throughout southeastern Asia.

Christianity: The religion founded in Palestine by Jesus Christ in the first century AD. It has spread into parts of Asia and throughout much of the western world.

French Indochina: The former French colonies centered upon Vietnam, Kampuchea, and Laos.

Islam: The religion founded in Arabia by Mohammed in the seventh century AD, whose founders are called Muslims. It has spread throughout the Middle East and southern Asia.

Judaism: The religion of the Jews, the ancient Hebrew people and their descendants, who have carried their religion to most countries of the world.

Mesopotamia: An ancient country between the rivers Tigris and Euphrates, now part of Iraq.

Mongols: A people, now living chiefly in Mongolia, who, in the thirteenth century AD, conquered the larger part of Asia.

Mughals: The Mongol rulers of India during the sixteenth to eighteenth centuries.

Nomads: Races or tribes with no permanent homes who move from place to place, sometimes across borders, according to the food or grazing available.

Palestine: An ancient Roman province on the eastern Mediterranean, a part of which was ruled by Britain from 1918 to 1947, now divided between Israel and Jordan.

Roman Empire: The empire established by the Romans in the first century BC. Between the fourth and fifteenth centuries, many countries of the Middle East and much of Turkey were ruled from the empire's eastern capital, Constantinople.

Romans: In this book, this word always refers to the Roman Empire, its armies, and its settlers.

Semites: Arabs, Jews, and some other races descended from ancient peoples who used a common group of languages.

Shiite: One of the two major religious divisions of Islam; the other is Sunni.

Sunni: One of the two major religious divisions of Islam; the other is Shiite.

Turkestan: A vast region in western and central Asia embracing several Soviet republics and parts of Afghanistan and China.

Turkic: A group of languages that includes Turkish.

Turks: Turkic-speaking peoples from Turkestan who founded the Seljuk and Ottoman empires.

World War II (1939-45): A war in which Britain, France, Russia, the United States, and their allies fought against Germany, Italy, Japan, and their allies. This war was fought mostly in Europe and the Pacific, but also in Russia, the Middle East, and the Far East.

INDEX

PICTURE ACKNOWLEDGMENTS — Arab League 8, 9 (lower), 13, 25, 29; Bodleian Library 12, 49, 61; R. Bonnett 45; British Library 17, 40; Food and Agriculture Organization (F. Mattioli) 22, 35, 47; Government of India Tourist Office 30; Hong Kong Tourist Board 48 (lower), 52; Indian Tourist Board 32, 33; Iraq Embassy 24; W. Irvine 41; Jordan Ministry of Tourism and Antiquities 9, 10, 11; Kuwait Ministry of Information 28; Lebanese National Council of Tourism 16; North Korea National Museum 53; Novosti 57; Oman Embassy 18; South Korea National Tourism Corporation 54; Sara Steel 6, 14, 23, 26, 34, 38, 39, 43, 56 (both), 59 (both); Thailand Information Service 44; Turkish Tourist Board 4, 5; UNESCO 20, 21, 36, 48 (upper); Young Library 51.